LEE EVANS ARRANGES HAROLD ARLEN

Photo Courtesy of ASCAP

ISBN 0-7935-3343-0

A Joint Publication of
MPL COMMUNICATIONS, INC.
and
HAL•LEONARD™

EXCLUSIVELY DISTRIBUTED BY

HAL•LEONARD™ CORPORATION
7777 W. BLUEMOUND RD. P.O. BOX 13819 MILWAUKEE, WI 53213

LEE EVANS ARRANGES HAROLD ARLEN

CONTENTS

FOREWORD

Harold Arlen's unique harmonies, melodies and rhythms, like those of George Gershwin and Stephen Sondheim, are distinguishing and distinctive characteristics of his music. This distinctiveness poses a difficult challenge to the arranger, who faces the dilemma of deciding how much of the composer's conception to retain in an arrangement if the integrity of the original is to be honored. (Indeed, the question of the necessity of retaining the integrity of the original in an arrangement or adaptation is an entire subject in itself.)

This writer is of the opinion that Arlen was the equal of Gershwin in terms of the mastery and range of jazz elements and expressiveness in his music, not to mention the quality of the songs themselves. Thus after a preliminary study of the song material in preparation for this book, I came to the inescapable conclusion that the more of Harold Arlen's writing I utilized in my arrangements, the better both the composer and performer would be served. The reader will quickly discover that this book is more Harold Arlen than it is Lee Evans (and frankly that's not easy for an arranger to do, as I learned during the creation of one of my favorite books, *Lee Evans Arranges Stephen Sondheim* for solo piano, which posed the identical challenge.)

Without trying to split hairs, this, then, is more often a book of solo piano re-creations than one of arrangements. Instead of naming the book *Lee Evans Arranges Harold Arlen,* perhaps it should have been called *Lee Evans Re-creates Harold Arlen.*

What I attempted to accomplish with this volume was to re-introduce pianists to the wonderful musicality of this genius of popular song, by stirring his musical juices into a fresh and revitalized, yet fairly faithful, pianistic presentation.

Lee Evans

OUT OF THIS WORLD
(From the Motion Picture "OUT OF THIS WORLD")

Lyric by JOHNNY MERCER
Music by HAROLD ARLEN
Arranged by LEE EVANS

MY SHINING HOUR
(From "THE SKY'S THE LIMIT")

Lyric by JOHNNY MERCER
Music by HAROLD ARLEN
Arranged by LEE EVANS

Ad-lib ballad style; plaintively and sensitively

Verse

Chorus

espressivo
mp

THE MAN THAT GOT AWAY

(From the Motion Picture "A STAR IS BORN")

Music by HAROLD ARLEN
Lyric by IRA GERSHWIN
Arranged by LEE EVANS

LET'S FALL IN LOVE
(From the Motion Picture "LET'S FALL IN LOVE")

Words by TED KOEHLER
Music by HAROLD ARLEN
Arranged by LEE EVANS

Semplice (circa ♩ = 84) (Straight 8ths)
Verse

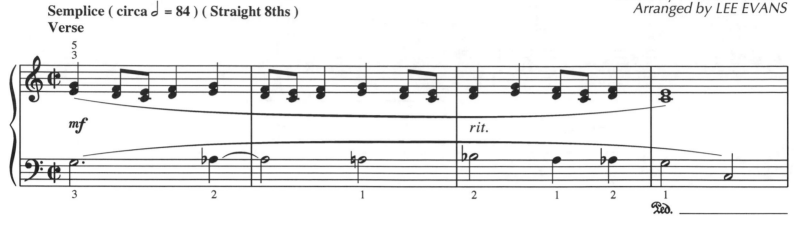

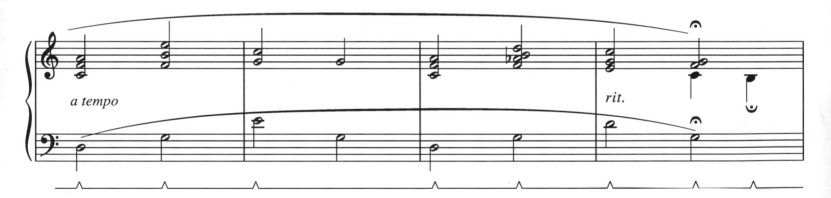

Easy Swing (♩ = 69) (♫ played as ♩³♪)
Chorus

THE MORNING AFTER

Lyric by DORY LANGDON
Music by HAROLD ARLEN
Arranged by LEE EVANS

Sensitively; ballad style (♩ = 48) (Straight 8ths)

Chorus

HOUSE OF FLOWERS

(From "HOUSE OF FLOWERS")

Lyric by TRUMAN CAPOTE and HAROLD ARLEN
Music by HAROLD ARLEN
Arranged by LEE EVANS

Moderato; freely; ballad style (Straight 8ths)

ONE FOR MY BABY
(AND ONE MORE FOR THE ROAD)
(From "THE SKY'S THE LIMIT")

Lyric by JOHNNY MERCER
Music by HAROLD ARLEN
Arranged by LEE EVANS

Lazily (♩ = 76)

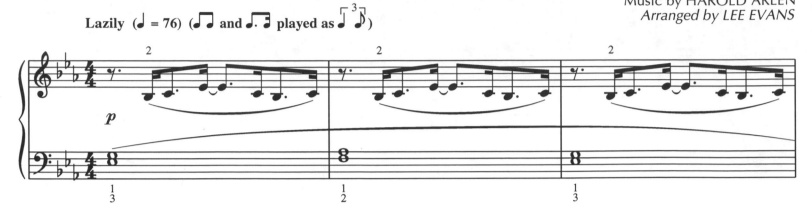

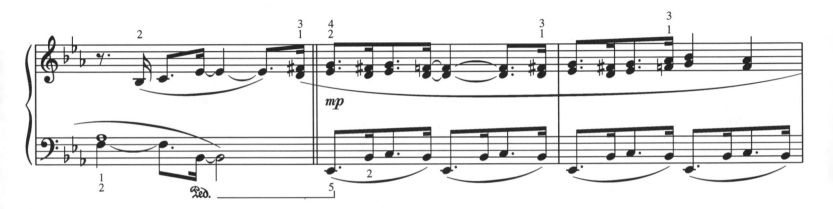

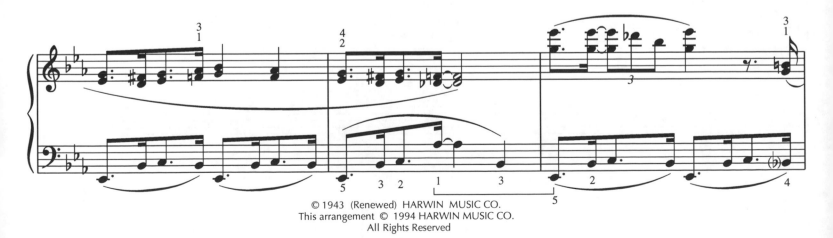

RIGHT AS THE RAIN

Words by E.Y. HARBURG
Music by HAROLD ARLEN
Arranged by LEE EVANS

A SLEEPIN' BEE
(From "HOUSE OF FLOWERS")

Lyric by TRUMAN CAPOTE and HAROLD ARLEN
Music by HAROLD ARLEN
Arranged by LEE EVANS

I NEVER HAS SEEN SNOW

(From "HOUSE OF FLOWERS")

Lyric by TRUMAN CAPOTE and HAROLD ARLEN
Music by HAROLD ARLEN
Arranged by LEE EVANS

In narrative style; freely (Straight 8ths)

Slowly and steadily ($\bullet$ = 40)
(Straight 8ths)

Interlude

TWO LADIES IN DE SHADE OF DE BANANA TREE

(From "HOUSE OF FLOWERS")

Lyric by TRUMAN CAPOTE and HAROLD ARLEN
Music by HAROLD ARLEN
Arranged by LEE EVANS

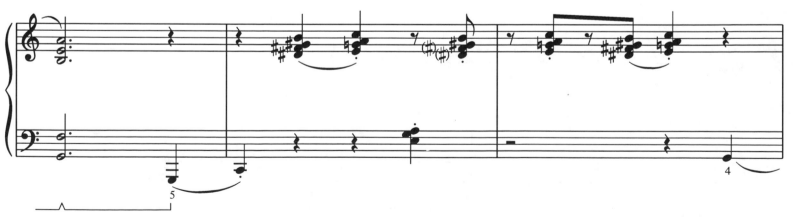

PARIS IS A LONELY TOWN

(From "GAY PURR-EE")

Lyric by E.Y. HARBURG
Music by HAROLD ARLEN
Arranged by LEE EVANS

THAT OLD BLACK MAGIC
(From the Paramount Picture "STAR SPANGLED RHYTHM")

Words by JOHNNY MERCER
Music by HAROLD ARLEN
Arranged by LEE EVANS

Rhythmically; with expression (♩ = 84) (♫ played as ♪♪)

STORMY WEATHER
(KEEPS RAININ' ALL THE TIME)
(From "COTTON CLUB PARADE" - 22nd Edition)

Lyric by TED KOEHLER
Music by HAROLD ARLEN
Arranged by LEE EVANS

WHEN THE SUN COMES OUT

Lyric by TED KOEHLER
Music by HAROLD ARLEN
Arranged by LEE EVANS

With a moderate beat (♩ = 100)

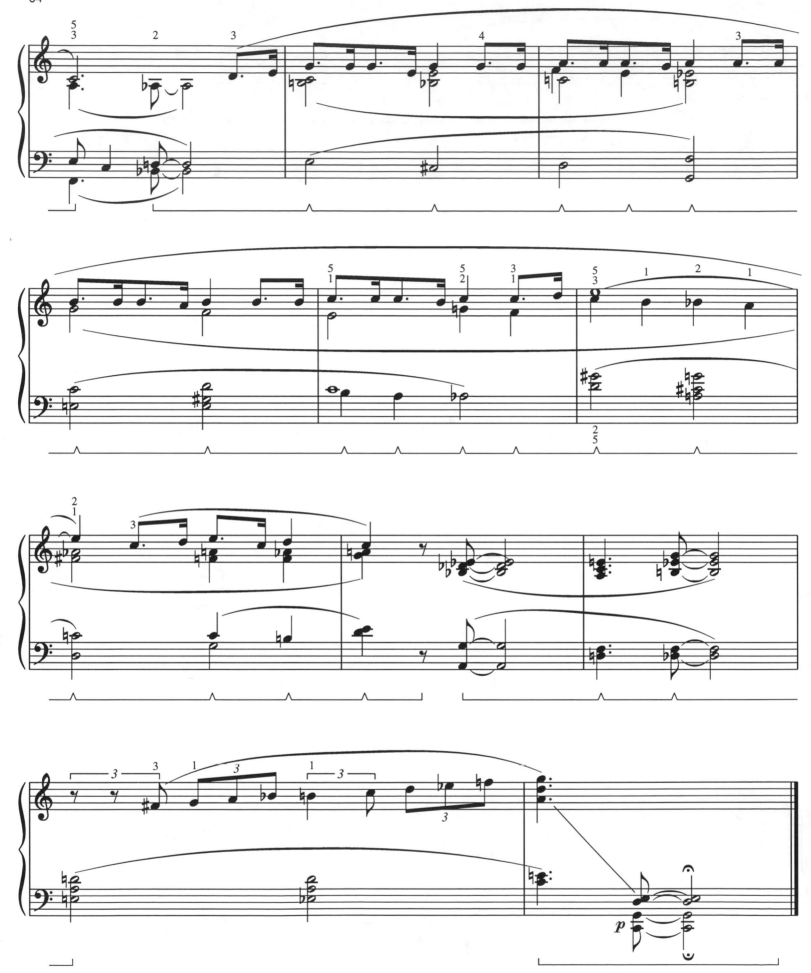

THIS TIME THE DREAM'S ON ME
(From the Motion Picture "BLUES IN THE NIGHT")

Words by JOHNNY MERCER
Music by HAROLD ARLEN
Arranged by LEE EVANS

HOORAY FOR LOVE
(From the Motion Picture "CASBAH")

Lyric by LEO ROBIN
Music by HAROLD ARLEN
Arranged by LEE EVANS

Jauntily and gracefully (♩ = 88)
Verse

IT WAS WRITTEN IN THE STARS

(From the Motion Picture "CASBAH")

Lyric by LEO ROBIN
Music by HAROLD ARLEN
Arranged by LEE EVANS

FOR EVERY MAN THERE'S A WOMAN

(From the Motion Picture "CASBAH")

Lyric by LEO ROBIN
Music by HAROLD ARLEN
Arranged by LEE EVANS

Seductively (♩ = 40) (Straight 8ths)

*Note: This arrangement follows the original sheet music quite faithfully. The original sheet, however, appears with a key signature of one flat, which is obviously incorrect. The arranger has reset the piece in four flats, reflecting the general F minor quality of the composition (although technically the work is in F Dorian Mode which takes a key signature of the three flats – B♭, E♭, A♭).

GET HAPPY
(From "SUMMER STOCK")

Lyric by TED KOEHLER
Music by HAROLD ARLEN
Arranged by LEE EVANS

ILL WIND
(YOU'RE BLOWIN' ME NO GOOD)
(From "COTTON CLUB PARADE" - 24th Edition)

Words by TED KOEHLER
Music by HAROLD ARLEN
Arranged by LEE EVANS

Meno mosso

I'VE GOT THE WORLD ON A STRING

(From "COTTON CLUB PARADE" - 21st Edition)

Words by TED KOEHLER
Music by HAROLD ARLEN
Arranged by LEE EVANS

AC-CENT-TCHU-ATE THE POSITIVE

(From "HERE COME THE WAVES")

Lyric by JOHNNY MERCER
Music by HAROLD ARLEN
Arranged by LEE EVANS

FANCY FREE
(From the Motion Picture "THE PRETTY GIRL")

Lyric by JOHNNY MERCER
Music by HAROLD ARLEN
Arranged by LEE EVANS

With great spirit (circa ♩. = 72) (Straight 8ths)

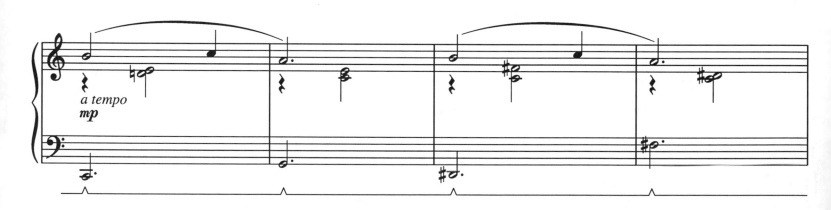

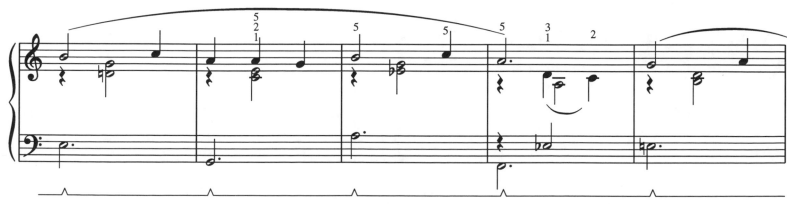

BLUES IN THE NIGHT
(MY MAMA DONE TOL' ME)
(From "BLUES IN THE NIGHT")

Words by JOHNNY MERCER
Music by HAROLD ARLEN
Arranged by LEE EVANS

BETWEEN THE DEVIL
AND THE DEEP BLUE SEA

(From the Musical Production "RHYTHMANIA")

Lyric by TED KOEHLER
Music by HAROLD ARLEN
Arranged by LEE EVANS

In narrative style; rubato (circa ♩ = 48) (Straight 8ths)

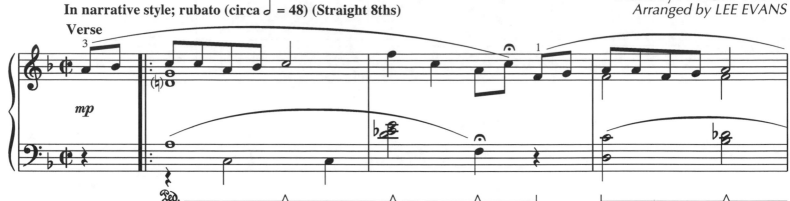

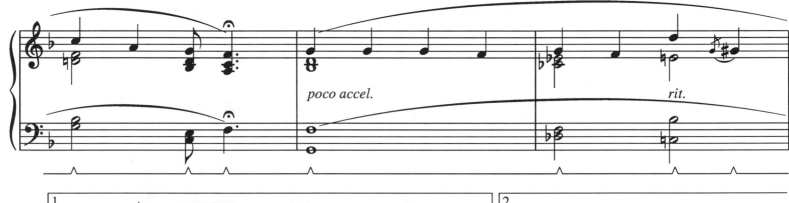

With a beat (♩ = 84) (♪♪ and ♩.♪ played as ♩♪)

COME RAIN OR COME SHINE

(From "ST. LOUIS WOMAN")

Words by JOHNNY MERCER
Music by HAROLD ARLEN
Arranged by LEE EVANS

Slow blues feel (♩ = 92)

I GOTTA RIGHT TO SING THE BLUES

(From the Musical Production "EARL CARROLL'S VANITIES")

Words by TED KOEHLER
Music by HAROLD ARLEN
Arranged by LEE EVANS

I HAD A LOVE ONCE
(From "CLIPPETY CLOP AND CLEMENTINE")
(An unproduced musical for television)

Words and Music by
HAROLD ARLEN
Arranged by LEE EVANS

I HAD MYSELF A TRUE LOVE

(From "ST. LOUIS WOMAN")

Words by JOHNNY MERCER
Music by HAROLD ARLEN
Arranged by LEE EVANS

IT'S ONLY A PAPER MOON

(From the Musical Production "THE GREAT MAGOO")

Words by BILLY ROSE and E.Y. HARBURG
Music by HAROLD ARLEN
Arranged by LEE EVANS

Rhythmically($\boldsymbol{\sqcup}$ = 76) ♫ and ♪. ♪ played as ⌐3⌐ ♪ ♪)

Chorus